Chelsea and Rachel are my go-to resource for all things Shopify. In fact, these two have become invaluable thought partners. From website tweaks and ReCharge implementation to email marketing and general strategy questions, they're on top of it. They never over promise, but they sure do over deliver!"

— JENNIFER KRUPEY, CALIFLOURFOODS.COM

This past year has been one of forced evolution for brands: it's become Direct to Consumer or Die. Fortunately, Chelsea and Rachel are here to help us all lose our tails and come out of the trees when it comes to this hard-to-understand discipline.

— JEFF KLINEMAN, EDITOR-IN-CHIEF
BevNET.COM, INC.

We are a really small resource-strapped team working on a fast-growing brand. ALOHA had this super complex, customized Shopify Theme that we couldn't use without engineers. (We couldn't make changes, updates, run smart promotions, etc.) We needed something more like paint by number and Chelsea and Rachel fulfilled that promise. My team actually has fun with Shopify now!

— STEVEN GMELIN, ALOHA.COM

SIMPLE
ECOMM~NOMICS

BRIDGING ECONOMICS AND
ECOMMERCE BEYOND 2020

CHELSEA JONES

RACHEL SAUL

COPPER CANOPY PRESS

COPYRIGHT

Summary: Want to improve eCommerce sales? This book is for you if you'd like a diverse portfolio of sales strategies... a responsive list of buyers... and a clear path between the two. Get the core concepts we've tested and optimized for our enterprise brand clients and specific implementation steps for growth mapping (while staying scrappy), market differentiation and messaging, sales through a subscription model, developing mobile first personalization, specific sales strategies, and more.

Here are the five pillars of success, and the blueprint for building them.

CONTENTS

To my family Ariella and Titus: Thank you for always being there and supporting me through thick and thin. We've finally launched a book! So grateful for you enduring tireless long nights and days for this to happen.

Thanks to Rachel for being a constant in my life, my business partner, and friend.

—Chelsea

To my husband Ryan and kids Johnny, Ruthy, Levi and Naomi - thank you for enduring the long nights and tireless days to help me get where we are today.

Thanks to Chelsea: Ditto! and helping me realize the childhood dreams I never thought would come true. Our shared values allow us to do business with gratitude, peace of mind, and hope.

—Rachel

INTRODUCTION

If we've learned anything from the pandemic of 2020, it's that change is fast, and it's constant.

Even during change you can prosper with some very specific principles we'll share in this book. If you want your company to actually thrive, your basic practices have to be more than basic. When you understand and implement these tactics, you will be unstoppable.

We are living in the most uncertain economic time in history. Your first path to success is knowing your customers, then making them happy. When you're able to talk with them directly, everything in your business gets easier.

Owning your customer data means you control sales. Direct access to your customers is the only way to widen your influence in the market.

That's what we want for you: a diverse portfolio of sales strategies... a responsive list of buyers... and a clear path between the two.

EXACTLY how that happens is inside this book.

You'll get the core concepts we've tested and optimized for our enterprise brand clients. Then you'll get specific implementation steps for:

- growth mapping (while staying scrappy)
- market differentiation and messaging
- sales through a subscription model
- developing mobile first personalization
- specific sales strategies

and more.

We'll show you five pillars of success, and the blueprint for building them. Although you may be most interested in branding, marketing, or eCommerce strategy, progressing through the pillars in order will prepare you for exponential growth.

There are some very specific instructions in this book. We've included these implementation steps because one small tweak in your branding message could make all the difference... streamlining overlapping applications could smooth store functionality and make it easier for your customer to purchase.

The market is always changing, and you can respond once you understand how to adapt to the market with principles that never change. Despite technology that evolves rapidly, these essentials apply to every product, in every industry.

Pillar One begins with a map for strategic growth. Let's get started!

PILLAR ONE: CUSTOMER JOURNEY MAPPING

To Grow, Know Your Numbers

In order to scale, you need more than website traffic. It's about the conversion rates along the path to checkout. At the end of this chapter there's a printable checklist to help you analyze your conversions.

This may sound too basic, but there's a good reason we're starting here. Your sales strategy is not designed once then put on auto-pilot. Your marketing needs to flex and change with the market. (There is no "one-size-fits-all.") To create a strategy, you start somewhere, then project forward. This is the map that grows you from where you are now.

Our clients typically want to increase their Average Order Value (AOV) or create repeat and subscription business. We've taken hundreds of small and enterprise brands through this process, and it all starts with this quick analysis.

Let's begin with your storefront analytics dashboard. (For all the examples in this book we'll use Shopify.) This has your indicators for engagement, growth, and success. While your revenue numbers seem most important, there are other factors in your predictive model that will make sure you're still around in five years.

You need to know *how your traffic converts into sales*. Where does that traffic come from, how consistent is it, and what's your revenue per channel? This is the way analytics reveal opportunities for growth.

Keep Testing Your Marketing

Advertising spend is the go-to solution for sales slowdowns, but it's not always the correct strategy. You have to think holistically and still be scrappy. Ads that worked last month may never work again. A "testing" mentality is the only way to move ahead as demand shifts, fulfillment changes, and supply chain issues crop up. *Something* is always changing.

So how do you engage, surprise, and delight your customer? How do you cross-sell and upsell so the purchase feels like a win for your customer and they don't feel they've been "sold"?

You create a meaningful interaction through your design engagement.

First, review the flow from your online storefront through the shopping process and on to checkout. Try to look at this as a new customer might see your website, hover their mouse, and click on navigation bars.

Remember that your customer wants a quick product description, then two clicks to checkout.

Getting Repeat Business

Clear and simple navigation improves sales, assuming a great product that ships on time. Fancy animations and beautiful graphics seem like a great idea, but only if they create a User Experience (UX) that keeps shoppers in your store all the way through checkout. So any spending on User Interface (UI) should increase your AOV, and convert customers into subscribers. Otherwise, it's extraneous.

To understand how all this comes together for your own business analysis, here's what might distract you: website visitors and conversion rates.

Yes, you need visitors to convert into sales, and there's still more to know.

What's your cost per lead (CPL)? How much are you spending to create a purchase? This number shows which customer acquisition methods are profitable, and which can be scaled up. It also points out where ad spend might be reduced or eliminated.

This doesn't automatically mean you should eliminate the more expensive CPL methods when those methods still bring new business. There are no strict rules when your ads create sales. You'll always respond to market changes, and monitor sales daily.

We mentioned engagement earlier, which really means how your visitors convert into sales. When someone clicks on your site, you immediately show visitors your product (without scrolling) and a fast path to checkout.

Keep It Simple

We cannot overstate the importance of simplicity in your online store.

The most common mistake is offering too much, or content that doesn't relate to the customer's story. There are overly long product descriptions, or founder stories placed ahead of product links. Focused problem-solving is what you should offer your store visitor.

Customers should see solutions first when landing on your page. They need to know how your product will help them as soon as they see your site. Their family may require their attention or a text could pull them from your store, then you've lost that sale.

If you have a food brand, the most visited page is your ingredients list, where you describe how it's made, or the benefits of your product.

Landing Page Views

The other vital statistic is your landing page view count. This determines if your ad is pulling the customer all the way through to checkout. You don't want to pay for clicks that go nowhere. These two numbers (landing page view and clicks on your ad) should be nearly the same.

To correct any discrepancies, check to see if your website is running slow. If load times are long, you will lose shoppers. Be sure your store is optimized for mobile browsing, and check your store link every day. Yes, every day.

Add-ons and Apps in Your Store

Here's a shocking truth: Your third-party platforms, coding, and apps might actually slow your site down.

As you continue to analyze your performance numbers in your store dashboard, the third area to review is the code inside your storefront. We often see apps piled on top of apps, and we understand how this happens... you're promised a pop-up lead capture, a one-click checkout, or another shiny shortcut to a sale. Before long, the store gets glitchy and it can even crash your site.

If a shopper hits a slowdown in your store front, they will leave without hesitation. You've worked too hard to get them to your store for a little glitch to take them out. Visit and test your store on every type of device; your mobile phone, tablet, and your desktop computer. Don't rely solely on the store's simulated view. You must check the actual store operation. Use an incognito browser so your cookies don't interfere with a fresh experience of your store.

Your Store Analytics Checklist

To get the most from this book and everything we know, go through this checklist and write down your analysis. Don't skip this step.

- How many store visitors do you have in a week and a month
- What's the sales rate versus visitor rate (conversion)
- What is your repeat business
- What are the referring sites

- Top product sold
- Last month's total sales
- Year-to-date sales
- Total sales itemized by lead source
- Cost per lead
- Source of sales from organic traffic
- Sales from paid ads
- Ad spend, and return on ad spend (ROAS)

You'll find a printable version of this Store Analytics Checklist in our **Bonus Content** at

https://chelseaandrachel.com/book-bonus/

Recap: Do These Three Things Every Day for Success

To distill the numbers into action steps, we're covering your essential daily tasks early in the book. This is how successful business owners focus their attention on the big picture of their business:

1. Marketing
2. Sales
3. Fulfillment

For the marketing task, it's great if the business owner can share something personal in their social channel, or write an email message that grows the connection with customers. As we just discussed, checking the analytics dashboard is the other essential part of each day.

In sales, you must check technology (or delegate the task) to be sure checkout is fully operational. There's nothing worse than customers who cannot complete their purchase.

The third daily task is monitoring demand and ensuring orders are filled and going out on time. Is staff keeping up, or are adjustments needed to keep things running perfectly?

If any one of these is off, you won't be able to scale and grow.

In the next section, we'll cover your brand strategy and how to stand out in a crowded market.

2

PILLAR TWO: BOOST YOUR BRAND

How do you stand out in the crowd and still look like you're in the right place?

You create a brand strategy that gives your customers a reason to buy.

Once you have the ideas and words to describe this, your visual representation communicates this through your

- logo
- color palette
- fonts, and
- website design elements

Branding is the first experience your prospects and customers have with you. A strong brand attracts your ideal customer, and pushes away people who don't align with your values and mission. In marketing, we know that everyone is not your customer. You need to speak directly to the market segment who is most interested in your product.

Who is Your Customer?

Calling out to your audience and future customers this way also repels people who aren't a good fit. This is proven now that we can drive inbound traffic based upon purchasing behaviors and demographics. Your branding is the first thing your prospects see about you. We need to quickly draw them in with a clear message and purpose.

What we know about website design and development allows us to test and improve brand strategy. From a broad perspective, your brand says who you are. Even more importantly, your product solves a specific problem for your customer. The essence of branding is a feeling, and you want your customer to enjoy your product.

The logo for Bobo's Baked Goods (eatbobos.com) demonstrates a specific feeling. You can also see the logos in our **Bonus Content** at

https://chelseaandrachel.com/book-bonus/

The mom waving her oven mitt is a simple line drawing that feels both unassuming and approachable. Some products show her smiling with her eyes closed. It feels like someone who enjoys taking good care of her family.

Sometimes the hype around the branding process means that simple strategies are overlooked. Owners believe sophistication is needed when simplicity is often best.

If we talked about messaging for an imaginary company who makes cookies, that could seem like a challenge as cookies have mass appeal and the market is broad. (Because who doesn't eat cookies?!)

Your brand tells how your cookie tastes, how you feel when you eat it, and how it's unique in the market. This messaging needs to be adjusted as time goes by and as markets change.

If you started making cookies because your daughter can't have gluten or dairy, share that story. Tell the "why" behind your mission so we understand your commitment to that product or audience group. Show them the happy outcome when they work with you and purchase your product.

Share the Story of YOU

The best brands lead with a story. Stories pull connection and create affinity. When you meet someone new and find you have something in common, you visit with them longer. This means there's trust from the beginning.

This is what you want your brand to do for you.

Branding is not about being popular or copying competitors, it's sharing the real you. That's how you find the clients and customers who need you most.

Reach Out to Your Customers

The market is always changing because people are changing. They're becoming more brand loyal and less location (or shopping place) loyal. Digital marketing must be specific and strategic. If you can get customers to engage with you directly, you can grow your sales and create subscriptions.

In fact, this is the only way your company will still be here in five years. You need direct interaction with your audience and customers.

Knowing what they want is how you anticipate changes in the market. Knowing their patterns of consumption (because you see individual orders through your subscriptions) is the best way to grow.

Success is a Moving Target

Want to improve your marketing message? Get the language of how your customers experience your product directly from them, and adjust your market messaging continuously.

Many owners and brand managers feel once they've nailed the profile of their perfect customer, they just need to pour more marketing dollars into targeting that specific avatar.

Only through direct interaction with your future customers (audience) will you understand what they're hoping to experience with your product. You cannot project your own thoughts and feelings onto your customer. Of course you're a consumer of your own product, but you may also be too close to it.

This direct to consumer approach requires the beginner's mindset. Continuous contact with your market over time is the only way to keep that mindset. All too quickly we see owners become experts (as they should) then lose their passion for experimenting. They believe it's all been figured out, and the problem is solved.

Knowing your market is essential, and that's why we wrote this book. We want you to understand that your audience is more than understanding your customer; it's a moving target.

When you're at the beach, you see waves breaking on the shore. It happens consistently, over and over, and you expect the salt spray. You know how to stand against the force of the breakers, and how to swim into calm spots. With marketing, we've seen companies become over-confident with their swimming abilities. They forget about the modulations and how things constantly shift, even if it's just inches in one direction. Soon they're off course and don't know how it happened.

We want more for you and for your customers. We want you to be here for a long time, providing the best product and best customer experience possible. Embrace the idea that your market is a moving target, always in the process of churning. It's a series of breaking waves that look the same, but require small shifts to maintain your market position.

Aloha.com clearly explains how this works; our clients had a clear social media presence and specific brand feel, even without their website being updated to match their social media.

When customers clicked through to their store site, it didn't feel like they were even visiting the same company. Because the colors and images didn't match social media, people felt disconnected from the experience they'd just had. This created confusion and low sales conversions.

It was exciting for us to have the opportunity to further optimize a great brand name like "Aloha." The white web page backgrounds were the perfect backdrop to shift and optimize the user experience inside their store. (You can also see Aloha's colors and logos in our **Bonus Content** at

https://chelseaandrachel.com/book-bonus/

> *Chelsea and Rachel worked closely with us and their team brought us along every step of the way. They made sure that we knew what they were creating for us, and how to use it. They built us this super sleek car, gave us the keys, and showed us it's as easy as driving a Camry (even though it turns heads like a Lamborghini.) – Steven Gmelin, Director of Digital @Aloha.com*

Your Branding Message Checklist

Now that you understand the why of branding, let's get into specifics. Here's a checklist to review how your brand communicates. (To get the most out of exploring these questions, imagine you don't yet have a logo and you're starting from the beginning.)

1. What problem does your product or service solve? Why would someone buy it?

2. What problem behind the problem are you really solving?

3. Do you have a special or unique story to share?

4. How do you create your products? Where did you learn to make them?

5. Write down everything that makes your product special. (Include basic things that you assume your competitors also do, but things that an industry outsider wouldn't know.)

6. What are your top values – your operating principles?

7. Write five adjectives or words that best describe your ideal customer and why they would buy from you?

8. What 20 keywords and key phrases does your potential customer use to find you in an internet search?

To make this easy, set your timer for twenty minutes and write as much as you can in the time you have. Now with the eye of a brand manager, review your current branding and look for ways to deepen your engagement. Could you share more of your origin story? Perhaps add some nuances about the inspiration for starting your company?

You'll find a printable version of Your Branding Message Checklist in our **Bonus Content** at

https://chelseaandrachel.com/book-bonus/

How People SEE Your Brand

An important part of your brand identity is the visual presentation. You want the colors and images to communicate the story of the solution you provide. Your logo and website are not as much a banner you wave, but the feeling you want your customer to have when they choose your solution.

Thinking through the emotional journey of your customer is like a dance. Think about the feelings your customer has when they want a treat for their daughter who can't have oats or dairy. Imagine the amount of research required by that mom to find your cookie company. Make it as easy as you can for that one specific person to instantly see and understand what you do.

The logo, images, and colors you choose for your website communicate that emotional journey. This is where testing and branding updates come into play. We see our clients get into the weeds on this because spending a lot of money used to mean that things turned out well.

The reality, however, is that if it's simple, it's better. If it requires scrolling, scrolling, scrolling to understand what your website sells, reorganize it. Now that we have phones in our hands or pockets every minute of every day, digital overload is real. You must communicate quickly and clearly.

A good rule of thumb in branding is to use no more than three colors on your site, and no more than two different font styles. There should still be space between the elements on your site, for example between the text and the photos. If you have too much information, you will fatigue your shopper and they'll just give up on your website. If your brand name doesn't quickly explain what you sell, your images must do that for you.

You can see how all these factors make branding a dance. There's balance and agility required so their experience flows smoothly to the shopping cart.

For a simple Branding Planner you can use right now, go to https://chelseaandrachel.com/book-bonus/

Your Branding Appearance Checklist

Take a look at your logo, colors, store, and website to answer these questions.

1. Does your company name describe the product or service you offer? (If not, what is the common definition of the words in your company name? Are they aligned with your mission and values?)

2. Is your logo easy to understand and does it clearly relate to your product or service?

3. What mood or feeling do the colors on your store or website communicate?

- Warm colors (orange, red, yellow and their variations) reflect passion, happiness, and energy.
- Cool colors (blue, green, purple and variations) reflect reserved feelings, calm and relaxed.
- Pastel colors (pale versions of any color) reflect calm and lightness and are typically paired with warm and cool colors, or black and white.

4. How many colors do you have in your logo and on your website?

5. How many different font styles are on your website?

6. Do the fonts and colors add to the emotion you want shoppers to have when they consume your product or service?

7. Is there space between the elements on your website that encourage the flow of the eye toward products?

8. Is the navigation clear and simple with 2-3 clicks to find a product and put it in your cart?

Review your website in ten minutes or less. For an extra level of brand message research, look at your top competitors using this specific visual brand review. How are they communicating their stories, and are they effective?

For a simple Branding Planner you can use right now and a downloadable version of Your Branding Appearance Checklist, go to our **Bonus Content** at

https://chelseaandrachel.com/book-bonus/

Your Brand is the Solution You Provide

Review your brand's words and images twice a year, whenever you change your market focus, or release a new product. When little things on your site are out of date, it creates confusion for your customer. Your website and storefront are the main method of communication, and dialogue with your audience should be current and continuous.

Just as you keep sending emails, your brand design is an ongoing strategy. Don't be afraid to make changes that better reflect who you serve. The more you share with your customers and clients, the more connected they feel to you. This also strengthens their loyalty to your brand.

If you go one step further and explain your logo and announce updates you make, your brand will attract more customers. They feel included when they understand why you choose to serve them and the story behind the story. Use that natural magnetism to deepen the connection with your audience and customers.

3

PILLAR THREE: EMAIL MESSAGING

Your email campaigns are an essential part of your e-Commerce success, and one of the core reasons we wrote this book. Your email list is how you communicate with your actual customer, so this part of your marketing must be done correctly.

The real surprise about your email strategy is that it's not about what you say in that email – it's about listening. Customer feedback is the best way to plan your success. What do they want? (They are your market, after all.)

When you keep in touch with your customer, you will refine products and processes. The business of selling begins by talking with customers about their needs and preferences like you did when you first opened your doors.

Staying scrappy means keeping one core strategy and serving your customer's needs. When you started your company, you focused on customer satisfaction. That will always be a primary goal for your business. Email between you and your customer is how you know what they want.

Own Your Data

The next step is to know your customer's name and email. While that may feel unusual to you at first, owning your customer's data is the right way to do business. It's something we feel strongly about based on our market experience.

Companies who rely on wholesale distribution (no matter how fantastic their product) lose business to the companies with the relationship to their end user. They have the name and email of their customer so they continuously improve their message and their product. *They effectively control the future of their company because of that direct communication with the customer.*

How to Create Email Relationships

Set up these five email automations to begin with:

1. Welcome to new subscribers
2. For shoppers who made a purchase
3. "Abandoned browsing" for those who were in your store but didn't make a purchase
4. "Abandoned cart" series if they selected items for purchase and never checked out
5. Cross-sell or up-sell
6. Promotions and special events

These emails are written ahead of time and loaded to send automatically when a prospect or customer takes one of the "trigger" actions. Your email service provider will use a sale or an initial opt-in to send out the emails in that series. This automation is sometimes called a "drip" campaign because you'll put several hours (or a day) between each email delivery action. The specific timing of delivery depends on which action triggered the email series.

Success in email is not the size of your list, it's about conversions. How many people open your email, then click the link, then make a purchase?

While this may seem too basic to mention here, building a small and engaged email list is better than a large list that doesn't buy your product. Don't be distracted by the wrong numbers.

Conversions always improve with more traffic. Do you have enough inbound traffic to make the numbers work? We'll talk about this more in Pillar Five, but this question always comes up when we discuss email campaigns. We wanted to seed the idea of traffic now because increasing traffic solves nearly every marketing issue.

What to Include in Your "Subscriber" Email Series

For the customers who enroll in subscriptions, you need an "update order" email. It goes out ahead of your specific shipping frequency; weekly, monthly, or other.

Here's where you encourage your customer to log into the shopping portal and make updates. Give them the opportunity to swap products or change quantities based on their actual consumption.

This is key to retaining your subscribers. If they have unconsumed product and their next shipment arrives, your customer is likely to cancel the entire service. In the customer's mind, they intend to sign up again once they run out of their current supply.

Having a "pause" option is important so cancellations don't happen simply because of communication issues.

While it seems counter-intuitive to ask your customer if they want to reduce or change their order, it's the best thing you can do. Not only are you sharing your genuine care and concern for your customer, you are going to make your customer happy and keep them in subscriber status when you offer opportunities to customize their shipments.

Good communication also prevents resentment. Offering an email reminder to further customize their auto-ship shows you care about the customer, not just "the sale."

Genuine care for your customer is how you build relationships. Relationships build loyalty. Loyal customers are happy, and continue to buy from you.

That's what we want for you as marketers. And that's what you want as a business... long-term happy clients who consume your product and tell their friends about you. Right?

Experiment with sending the "update order" opportunity email on different days of the week. Maybe Sunday works best for a while, and then it shifts to Saturday. You can also experiment with different offers they can add to their regular shipment.

What to Include in Your "Purchaser" Email Series

You also need a one-time purchase email series. The first email goes out to confirm the order, send a receipt, thank them, and build anticipation by confirming their purchasing decision was a good one.

This will validate their buying decision. Remind them of the promises made in your sales messaging to keep them excited about their new purchase. Always provide them with proof they made a great buying decision.

Reinforcing the reason they purchased is important once the "buy now" button is clicked. This can help minimize cancellations and returns.

The next email is an update on shipping status and package tracking.

The last email will ask about their experience with your product. Congratulate them on the result they're about to achieve and share some of the emotional responses or testimonials from your current customers. Continuing to sell in your follow-up email is standard practice because it's effective.

Sharing is Caring

You can also offer an incentive or bonus if they share their purchase on social media. Give them some ideas about how to use your product. If it's a cookie, create an image of an occasion or situation where they may never have thought to bring cookies before. Include a recipe for a specialty cookie treat, or how to use cookies in place of a celebration cake. Get creative with ways your product could be used and let them know you'll provide more tips in the future. New and unique approaches on product use will encourage social sharing.

If this purchase is not a subscription and they buy again, you want to respond and recognize those customers. Your thank-you email should let them know you noticed they came back, and you appreciate their return to your store. Stay in touch with every one of your customers.

After you've written those basic emails that confirm purchase and shipment, send them an offer to receive your email updates, a regular newsletter, or special promotions.

Finally, send an email asking for a product review in your store. Even though the automated sales process has a request for reviews built in, adding another request in your email series is a great reminder that will result in more reviews.

Checklist for Email Analysis

Here are the review items to be sure your email system is running at its best:

- Is there an email capture on your website's home page? (Triggered after 30 seconds of their first-time visit)
- Is there a pop-up box to capture email before they leave your website? (triggered upon clicking away from your site)
- Do you segment your list by product interest, or another method?
- Do you know the average order value from your email subscribers?

- Do you know which email subscribers are opening your emails, purchasing from that email, and which people never open any emails?

If you'd like to download your book bonus "7 Ways to Improve Email Engagement" as well as a printable version of this Checklist for Email Analysis, go to our **Bonus Content** at

https://chelseaandrachel.com/book-bonus/

4

PILLAR FOUR: YOUR WEBSITE ESSENTIALS

Let's talk about what's important on your website, and what to avoid.

Since this is a visual representation of what you do, the words on the page communicate the feeling your customer has when they consume your product. The entire strategy behind your website is to create a customer.

We've seen clients who hyperfocus on animation and beautiful logos, colors and graphics. Even when you're a market disruptor, this will distract your customer from getting to checkout. Being different is explained in your copy, not by breaking the standard rules of web design.

Shoppers are shoppers, and they expect a flow to the product page to checkout. Focus on the big picture of who you serve. What makes them happy about your product or service?

Initially, brand managers and owners think a website is how you position your brand to your audience. Kind of like a press release that needs to cover all the facts.

The truth is you have to zoom out a little. Your website is not a billboard. It's not an advertisement. Your website is an invitation.

Website Components

Before we give you our list of absolute musts, think of your potential customer Sarah. She's a busy mom who needs what you have; let's use coffee as an example.

She's tired, and wants a quality cup of coffee to set her up for a productive day with her family. She finds your site and wants to know how to get good tasting coffee that isn't too expensive, and wonders how soon it can be in her kitchen.

Sarah clicks on your site link, then on the shop button. There are different coffees listed, and the next click goes to a product description page. She scrolls down to see roast options, and wants to be sure it's ethically sourced.

Then her kid walks in and needs her. Sarah leaves her computer without putting anything in her cart. As the website owner, were you notified that Sarah visited? Did you send her another invitation to shop, or send a browse abandonment email?

Perhaps a message like "Hey Sarah, thanks for checking out our coffee! I know life gets busy, but don't forget your cuppa!"

You just missed an opportunity to personalize a visit and get your coffee into Sarah's kitchen. She was 3 clicks in and never made it to the shopping cart. You need the right triggers in place to stay in touch with that potential customer. Here's what you need to set up to maximize every sales opportunity:

- Live chat invitation - float in or pop up
- a quick "add to cart" pop up
- an offer to continue browsing that's triggered by an idle state

We have some favorite apps and services that we'll list for you at the end of the chapter.

Testing Website Design

Your website should have a simple design, then try it against another simple design.

Even popular Shopify templates need to be tested for the best response rates. You need to go through your user's story and mindset, and find the clearest way to explain the outcome of your product or service. If you're selling coaching, consulting, or courses, we suggest the Kajabi platform. If you offer consumer packaged goods (CPG) then Shopify is our favorite.

Once you've chosen your sales platform, you want to keep the plugins and apps to a minimum. You have to be strategic about every component you add to your site to maintain quick loading.

If you're considering a website redesign, download our decision tool "Is It Time to Rethink Your Website?" in our **Bonus Content** at

https://chelseaandrachel.com/book-bonus/

Instant Gratification

How often have you clicked away from a website because it didn't load and open in the first two seconds? This is a big issue in eCommerce, and this will cost you sales. Don't be dazzled by fancy graphics that will slow everything down. A simple path is always your priority.

There are several good apps we recommend to our clients for email capture and shopping carts. Those are also in the list at the end of this chapter. Please remember it's not an across the board recommendation because industries are different, and different products and price points require customization.

When someone visits your site, they expect to see the product they were searching for. Maybe they don't know exactly what they want yet, but they visited for a reason. You have to deliver on their wish for immediate answers.

How do you invite first time visitors and returning shoppers to find what they want quickly? You need to have your product catalog front and center. Let them find out about your company and your products, but spotlight the product.

Your returning shoppers also want to get to their cart quickly. Keep your products inside a catalog. Take a look at the website for Two Leaves and a Bud at twoleavestea.com. To see how we grouped their product catalog, go to our **Bonus Content** at

https://chelseaandrachel.com/book-bonus/

. . .

Having everything inside of categories creates a simple user experience. We want a clear navigation flow without presenting too many options. Just remember we want to give the visitor what they want as quickly as possible. Show them what's for sale!

Best Content on Your Website

Here are the pages you need for your website:

- Home page – this is your brand and links to your products
- Collection or Products page – lists items available for sale
- Contact page – how customers can reach you
- Policy page – includes your terms of service
- Shipping and Returns page – explains shipping, return and refund policies
- Founders page – describes the story for startup companies
- Brand or Mission page – why you're in business
- Ingredients page – for food and beverage companies
- Footer and Header – this is a site wide feature that provides navigation links to all the other pages in your site

For an additional resource "The Visual Guide to Website Content", visit our **Bonus Content** at

https://chelseaandrachel.com/book-bonus/

Necessary on Your Site

The functions you must have on your site include:

- Email lead capture
- Phone number capture (for SMS offers)
- Chat feature (available on each page in your site)
- Subscription option or package offer inside the shopping cart

Website Tools and Resources

- Klayvio: email and SMS platform
- Recharge: credit card and subscription processor
- Hotjar: Free service that reports user experience through a heat map
- Gorgias: a chat bot for creating customer service tickets and email replies
- Facebook messenger (ONLY if you don't use a chat bot, but don't use both)
- Rebuy: an in-cart upsell tool that includes a free gift option once your pre-determined cart value is reached

Checklist of DO and DO NOT from Our Senior Engineers

Our engineering team has more than 40 years of programming experience, and these are rules we grabbed directly from our workflow feedback channel.

. . .

Do Not:

- Use Hero Carousels (heat maps show most people aren't on that page for more than one slide; this feature only adds page weight with all the coding required. This affects your loading time and every split-second counts when someone visits your page.)
- Have navigation tab titles that are different than the page title (the "ABOUT" page should say "about" at the top, not "our story" or "this is us" or anything other than ABOUT)
- Fussy Animation (or on-page movement simply for the sake of being trendy. Does it add to the value of the page or is it taking attention from shopping?)
- Use Ghost Buttons as primary navigation buttons. (When the mouse hovers over, it's an outlined or ghost image.)
- Offer Social Links at the top of any page. (Social media is for bringing traffic in, not directing visitors away from your website.)
- Allow Pop-up boxes to cover your page content. Trigger them only when clicking away or after 30 seconds on the page.
- Add Unrelated Content. (Keep the user story clean and the path clear, don't distract your shopper.)

Do This Instead:

- Navigation and page tabs should be clear and simple.
- Have some engaging/fun image animations

where products move into the cart or into bags when shopping. Make shopping into a game that's super engaging.

- Every page on your site should have only one focal point: what's the most important thing you want your visitor to do on that page? (CTA in almost all cases.)
- Only live links and redirects should look like links. (Don't underline text that's not interactive.)
- Keep labels on your form fields like "name" and "email". (Don't eliminate the labels and rely only on the placeholder within that form.)

Other general advice from our engineers is to avoid design decisions based on the "fold" of the webpage because there's no way to know where it is for each user. (If you look at your phone normally, then turn it 90 degrees to landscape view, the "fold" changes dramatically.) Any text you can read on screen without scrolling is considered above the fold.

E-readers and wearable tech (like Apple watches) mean there's no one standard way that content is viewed. Website design is not the same as designing something for print.

Scrolling on a website is a fact of life. Site visitors expect to scroll, and will try to scroll even when a page has very little content. You don't need visual indicators to tell them to scroll.

The top of every page always needs a compelling headline or they won't read the body text. Give them a reason to stay and scroll with tight messaging, a clear unique selling proposition (USP) and vibrant product imagery.

To get the printable versions of The Website Content and Functions Checklist as well as the Website Tools and Resources, go to our **Bonus Content** at

https://chelseaandrachel.com/book-bonus/

5

PILLAR FIVE: ECOMMERCE

The Basics

To maximize your sales, you must widen your delivery channels so your infrastructure can support growth.

If you wanted to stay small, you would've rented retail space and served your zip code. Because you want to reach customers beyond your backyard, you went online. It's the only way to scale.

Online exposure will increase your brand awareness and introduce your products and services to people you haven't met yet. The simplicity of this concept cannot be overstated enough; your customers are individual people.

They are not a market, nor a demographic. They are a Chelsea and a Rachel, they are moms and sisters and daughters. Your customers have emotions and needs and distractions of their own.

If you always remember that your "market" is full of people like your own family, it will remind you that customers are also curious and ever-changing. This is why your marketing and your store front need to engage and excite. To sustain interest over time, it needs variety.

If you learn only ONE thing from this book, this is that one thing. Your customer is a real person with tastes and preferences that change over time. They are not a predictable or static "avatar", and selling is not simply a transaction. It's about understanding wants and preferences so you can deepen the relationship with your customer over time.

This mindset is your foundational marketing tool. When you remember your customers are real people like you and me, testing and experimenting with messaging becomes standard operating procedure.

Subscriptions Mean Success

This is the real key to longevity, and it's a foundational pillar for every eComm business.

Subscriptions mean you have repeat business and retain your customers. It will also increase your AOV and the lifetime value of your customer. In the food and beverage segment alone, subscriptions increase lifetime value 3.25X. (Source: ReCharge subscription services.)

Even companies who don't offer quick-turn consumable products need to offer subscriptions. It could be a digital offer like a monthly planner, or membership to content or a community. You could offer a gift option so they could purchase your product for someone else. There could be a monthly surprise box that pulls different items from the catalog, even if it were a three-month only option.

Another boost to retention is through the customer portal experience. Having a user name and password along with the ability to modify an order doubles the lifetime value of a customer.

Creating a custom experience for each subscriber is built into subscription software, which also reports the churn rate. That's the length of time someone stays subscribed, and it's important to note any patterns in subscription drop off.

The longer you collect data on this, the easier it is to craft marketing strategies to intervene before churn happens.

Sometimes that means an email goes out with an offer to swap products, or to change the timing of deliveries from two weeks to six weeks. Perhaps a text message goes out just before a customer reaches the point in your timeline you see cancellations occur. Now you can re-engage them with an insider tip, or let them know about a special that's only available at this point in their subscription timeline.

Monthly revenue becomes predictable when you increase your subscriptions. Your long-term projections become stable, and that helps you plan everything in your business from product development to staffing. Subscriptions are the real key to ongoing success.

Getting Google to Notice Your Store

Every word of text on your web page (also known as copy) is searched and indexed by Google. From your headlines to your footers, you want every word to explain what you offer your customer.

This will help your organic search rankings. When someone types "healthy nut-free bar" into their browser, your product image should ideally pop up.

Even now that most everyone has an online marketing budget, we're still asked how to get attention without ad spend. Not only is that a long and winding road, it's nearly impossible.

What we're going to cover here are the specific and critical components to move you toward enterprise level sales.

Which Website Pages to Optimize for Site Indexing

All of them? Yes.

It's not only the copy that your visitors read on the page, it's also what's on the meta data section behind-the-scenes on each page on your website.

Your first priority is your product page and the page title. Typically, we see the name of the product category listed as the page title (or the "meta title" depending on your hosting platform.) This is how you want to title your pages. You also want headlines on your customer-facing copy to vary from your meta data title.

This is where you can expand the description of your product category. If we use a healthy food example again, you'd have "collection-oat-bars" as the meta title name of your page, and your page title would say "baked oat bars".

In your Meta Description, you'd list some ingredients and mention vegan, soy-free, 100% organic, and the other words your customers are searching for.

Caution: Keyword Stuffing

If you've been around for a while, you've heard of keyword stuffing. At one time Google was rewarding sites that loaded keywords on their home page. Those sites were featured in organic searches. Times have changed, thank goodness. Keyword-loaded copy (similar to a keyword cloud) was not reader-friendly. It didn't explain the product or the service, or how it could help.

So how do you write your copy? Make your product pages and descriptions flow like a conversation. The way to connect with your customer is to make every-thing conversational. Short sentences are better so get to the point. Don't clog your page with flowery language or clever phrases because it's far too easy to give the wrong impression. Copy is interpreted by individuals who have life experience and their own sense of humor. What you think is funny may be seen as offensive to someone else.

Without making things too generic, your tone on the page should be as neutral as possible. It's kind of like staying out of politics and religion; stay focused on the results your product will provide.

Ad Spend Fundamentals

While every company is different, there are some principles that apply across the board. For example, your pay-per-click (PPC) spending should be at least

15% of your monthly sales goal. While a typical conversion rate for PPC is one percent, that's only a baseline. We've seen better numbers when the customer path to checkout is clear and just 2-3 clicks to get there.

Once our clients can analyze numbers for themselves, they can actively grow their sales. Checking the app for their store account allows daily review of the numbers, then leadership has the input they need to respond quickly.

This is what founders and managers do... analyze the data and make decisions for next steps. Mapping strategic growth begins with understanding your numbers.

Copy on Your Product Page

In the world of online stores, your page content cannot be shallow. This is when you have less than 300 words. There is always more you can say about your product, and this is where you say it.

If you've written everything you can think of and still have less than 300 words, here are some ideas:

- Talk about your manufacturing process and what you do differently.
- If you think your manufacturing is the same as everyone else, then explain one of the industry standards and why it's important to you. Share your point of view and your interest in your production process.
- Explain your sourcing values and why you've chosen those ingredients or that packaging.

- Share something from your R&D phase to reveal insider knowledge of this product.
- Mention part of your origin story here and share your passion for this product.
- Include your individual ingredients, your nutrition panel, or your product specifications.

If you can't get to 300 words no matter how hard you try, then that product needs to move in with another page where there's already existing copy.

To get the printable versions of "Copy on Your Product Page" and blog ideas, go to our **Bonus Content** at

https://chelseaandrachel.com/book-bonus/

Store Front Integration

Once you've listed all of your titles and descriptions on the metadata side of your pages, the Google shopping feed will add your site into their index. This will help you get discovered in keyword searches. Your online presence extends beyond your storefront. Every blog you post, podcast you guest on, and video you share should have your keywords and web address listed in the metadata.

This will allow you to track your keyword use and test its success, and select the media your customers best respond to. All of this is part of your ongoing increase in response, also known as "lift", over time.

Why Shopify?

When we formed Chelsea and Rachel Co. in 2014, it was after launching a successful Kickstarter product campaign in only three weeks. This is why Shopify continues to be our preferred platform. We loved the options and how easy it was to try different designs. Even today, our most successful clients continue to test and engage their market. They are the ones who win.

If you're getting caught up in shopping button design and colors, you are missing sales. Your store and website should be always changing, dynamic and flexible. It's not like checking off a list that's completed and never revisited.

The themes and modules inside Shopify will get you up and going faster. Of course, you can custom develop your store, but using their module format is typically the best start on Shopify.

You can edit sections of those modules to create something unique to your company and product. It offers long-term flexibility and functionality, and it's one of the most powerful technology stacks available.

As Shopify Plus Preferred Service Partners, we're one of only a handful of women-owned agencies in the U.S. who qualified for certification to help our clients build (and migrate) their store sites. There are only 200 of these partners worldwide who have passed Shopify's rigorous requirements for certification.

We also have a direct communication channel with Shopify. We are able to request features and get quick responses to issues. This means we keep our client stores running at their peak. The icing on the cake are the insider tips we get on what's working today in the market. This is why using an agency for digital marketing can shortcut your success; they have expertise and connections they've spent years acquiring.

Organic Traffic Success Through SEO

You can still generate leads and traffic without advertising dollars. That's what organic traffic does. Even with an enormous ad budget, you still need an SEO strategy so your social media and website content is indexed.

There are 30 different things we review with retainer clients to customize their plan, and we've included some of our best practices here for you.

First, select the page on your website that contributes most to product sales. Is it the *shopping* page or *products* page? That's where you focus your energy first.

Create a list of words that describe the content of the page, otherwise known as "keywords". You should be able to come up with 50 that could describe that product, its ingredient list, or its unique characteristics.

If you need inspiration to get your list to 50 terms, use Amazon and Wikipedia searches to help.

Next, log into your website and edit your page. In the "SEO" section there should be a place for the SEO meta title and meta description. This is where you add the words that describe your product.

You want just your top ten keywords here, not all 50. Use a keyword research tool like the Google Keyword Planner to see how many people search for that word or phrase. You also want the readable copy on your page to reflect those keywords.

Check your keyword performance weekly to adjust your ranking.

"How long to steep tea" is a winner for our client **Two Leaves and a Bud** even though it's a high volume, high competition phrase. We check and update their page content frequently so Google refreshes and maintains their top organic ranking.

Site Loading Speed

Next you need to check how quickly your webpage loads into a browser window. Gtmetrix.com is one of the places that will analyze your site performance for free and give you optimization suggestions.

If your website takes too long to load, your customer is going to click away. Ask your web developer to make the suggested fixes on your caching, image optimization, JavaScript, and everything that ranks below a grade of "B". Your site needs to be updated and checked weekly.

The tips we listed earlier from our engineers also affect site loading speed, and now you get to review your own site's performance with this free tool.

Your Page Titles and Section Subtitles

While you're inside the control panel of your website, click on the "text" tab on your page content. This lists your hierarchy of titles and subtitles, more accurately called headers. There are three header types, H1 through H3. This determines the size of the font, and also allows for web-crawling robots to add your titles to their indexes.

You want your headers to reflect your targeted keywords. Be sure to change your ALT tags on any images to reflect your keywords (instead of their original file names) since ALT tags are also indexed by bots.

When you have a collection of products, include the main keyword as part of your collection title. Your meta page title in the SEO section must include that same keyword.

A common mistake we see is using the same keywords for multiple pages inside a website. Each page should have its own unique keywords that aren't used on any other page. Indexing will ignore both pages if you use the same keywords in the SEO metadata.

Backlinks from Other Websites

When another website includes a link to your site, that contributes to domain authority and page trust. The indexing bots give your page a higher rank if other websites include a link to your site. They assume you have something to contribute, otherwise your site would not be linked on pages you don't own.

Now that voice dictation also uses search engines, spoken requests are also indexed on Google. This is considered to be a *long tail phrase*. Those are typically more than three words, or are asked in the form of a question.

If your header tags can be spoken as a question, that similar meaning will still be indexed even when the terminology is not identical.

Do You Have a Blog?

Here's where you write about your product. Each entry should be 300 words or more to catch the attention of the website crawlers. Your blog can educate your customers about specific topics related to your products, discuss client success and positive outcomes, and offer new ideas for your prospects.

Be sure to have a headline for your blog as well as section titles. Each of those heads and subheads are ranked in SEO searches.

If you have a blog post longer than 300 words, you can repurpose it. Create a downloadable PDF of that post, turn it into a slideshow, or create short excerpts for LinkedIn.

Each blog entry also requires metadata information. Even blog comments will contribute to the organic traffic search.

This is an often-overlooked strategy in online sales. Some companies mistakenly believe the product speaks for itself, and they ignore what a blog can do for them.

Your owner or founder can use the blog much like a press release venue. They could communicate weekly and give updates on the company as well as upcoming product releases. Someone else in the company could also write the blog and post it on behalf of the founder.

What's important is the continuous creation of new content. The more copy on your website, the more indexed search terms will help your site ranking. Each post should be unique, and that content cannot be published anywhere else online, or on any other page in your website.

If you need help creating content, a copywriter can help. We have staff to help us create content for our clients because the words on your page are important. Even if you start with one blog entry a month, that's better than zero. Put it on the calendar and work your way up to a weekly post.

What About Specific Niches and SEO?

The more niche you are, the easier it is for you to rank in SEO. When someone wants what you offer, they will type it into the search engine. If you don't have each page's metadata up to date with different keywords and phrases, you are missing key sales opportunities.

If you're in a highly competitive industry, you can still rank organically with the help of your blog. When we create a strategic site plan for new clients, we review every page and blog entry. We check the SEO ranking weekly and follow our internal optimization guidelines. This has been one of our clients' favorite services because it boosts cold traffic discovery without ad spend.

If you monitor your own SEO results, there are software services you can implement for $50 a month. That monthly report also makes specific suggestions on optimization. After being in business for nearly a decade, we know the SEO results are worth updating each week. It's much like building your own website at the beginning, then outgrowing what a web developer can implement for you. SEO is a specialty in itself and worth an investment of time and staff resources.

AFTERWORD

It's time to make a plan and get to work.

Imperfect marketing action beats no action any day. You can't modify your marketing until you've tried something and measured it. Rest assured, your marketing will never be perfect. It will be launched, but it's never finished.

Adopting this "test and experiment" mindset is the only true path to success. it will keep you curious and energized, knowing there's always an opportunity to improve. Now go and download our **Bonus Content** at

https://chelseaandrachel.com/book-bonus/

Go through each and every checklist, take action, and we promise your sales will improve. There's nothing that's impossible to implement here. If you don't have the knowledge or time to complete the steps in this book, then delegate it or hire someone to do it for you.

As a leader, business owner, or entrepreneur, you're the only one who can move the needle forward. Take this information and take action. Use the hashtag #CReComm to post your wins. Please email us at wins@chelseaandrachel.com with all your success stories.

We can't wait to see where you go next.

INVITATION FOR A STRATEGY CALL

If you'd like to discuss specific business questions, choose a time that works for you here:

https://go.oncehub.com/CR-7Figures

We'll also ask about your business goals for the next twelve months as well as your big dreams. Perhaps a small shift will get you there, or maybe a new action plan makes more sense.

Take advantage of our experience with enterprise level eCommerce and move strategically toward the right goals.

We look forward to hearing about you and your business.

ACKNOWLEDGMENTS

Jesus Christ Our Lord and Savior who has given us strength to carry out our mission. We thank The Bible for being a source of wisdom, and the core foundation of who we are.

Our kids who think that any food delivery is a care package from our clients.

Our parents Byron Hodge and Barbara Bourland, and Rod and Sandy Akins for instilling in us a drive and passion to be different (and always great) at what we do.

Kris Akins and Lynn Hessling for bringing us together on our first project of Charlie Curls.

Mark Reese for being with us from Day One as our longest standing client.

BevNET for the opportunity to speak and get our expertise in front of more incredible brands, and Jeff Klineman for your read-through of this book and your Editor-In-Chief help.

Bobo's and Mike Mackey for introducing us to the food and beverage segment, and for being the catalyst for becoming a leader in this market.

Jen from Cali-flour for believing in our potential and for introducing us to NatchCom.

ReCharge for being our favorite partner and always supporting our crazy endeavors. We can't do this without you. Shout out to Elaine for being AHmazing.

Shopify for creating a platform and inviting us to be Shopify Plus Preferred Service Partners: thanks to Katie, Nick and all the crew.

Steven Gmelin of Aloha for being not only a rockstar client, but our thought partner and connector.

Traffic and Funnels for challenging us to grow and put our dreams into action through mentoring and coaching.

Our team for believing in what we do, and upleveling and improving your skills constantly.

Barbara for being a rock and our agency "mom" and keeping our details in line. We couldn't function without you.

Christina Dreve for her book editing.

Apple computers for always working and never getting viruses.

InstaCart for revolutionizing our lives as working moms.

The privilege of traveling, and how it inspires us.

The ability to be athletic and run to keep our energy and output maximized.

For the time to process deep thought and strategy for ourselves as leaders.

Coffee. Thank you to all the coffee.

To the thought leaders:

Sally Hogshead for making us see life and business differently.

Simon Sinek for inspiring us to always lead with The Why.

ABOUT THE AUTHORS

Chelsea & Rachel Co. are Shopify Plus experts in designing and implementing digital marketing, and leveraging online platforms. Their expertise includes e-Commerce trends, functionality, customer behavior, and design. They've helped many businesses transform underperforming sites into all-out sales booms by simply improving the user's online shopping experience.

Chelsea Jones is a strategic direct-to-consumer expert and a professional problem solver for consumer brands. She has an extensive background in web design and development, as well as more than 14 years in advertising and graphic design. Chelsea leads with vision, explains specific tactics with clarity, and knows the why behind best practices.

Rachel Saul specializes in direct-to-consumer marketing and technical advertising strategies. With more than 16 years in the industry, she is an expert in UX/UI user story design, subscription strategy, digital marketing strategy, email marketing, and automation. Rachel works on structures where small changes have big impact.

Chelsea & Rachel Co. Team includes 18 talented individuals with focused experience as UX/UI graphic designers, highly-skilled front-end and full-stack web developers, content writers, photographers, videographers, SEO experts, project managers, email marketers, and more.

CPSIA information can be obtained
at www.ICGtesting.com
Printed in the USA
BVHW092223280622
640819BV00013B/1289